PREFACE

1. Purpose

This publication provides fundamental tactics, techniques, and procedures (TTP) for planning, integrating and employing biometrics collection at the tactical level in support of operations. It provides guidance for collecting facial images, fingerprints, iris scans, deoxyribonucleic acid (DNA), and palm prints to maximize data quality. Adherence to procedures in this publication will improve the efficiency and effectiveness of identity operations, deny the enemy anonymity, and reduce risk to friendly forces.

Note: For the Army, the term "command and control" was replaced with "mission command". Mission command now encompasses the Army's philosophy of command (still known as mission command) as well as the exercise of authority and direction to accomplish missions (formerly known as command and control).

2. Scope

This publication provides a standardized multi-Service framework for planning, integrating, and employing biometrics data collection efforts by tactical units designed to improve data quality and maximize system capability in direct support of military operations. It provides small unit leaders and collectors a clear, fundamental understanding of the impact accurate and valid data has on the overall biometrics process. Also, it provides planning considerations for enrollment site selection and procedures designed to maximize data quality. This publication:

- Supplements established doctrine and TTP.

- Describes the impact of properly collecting biometrics on operations.

- Provides a detailed explanation of procedures.

- Provides information to effectively organize, plan, and execute biometrics data collection employment in a multi-Service environment.

3. Applicability

This MTTP publication applies to all commanders, staffs, and operators participating in biometrics collection operations. This publication is unclassified with public release and unlimited distribution, in accordance with Department of Defense directive 5230.24, *Distribution Statements on Technical Documents*.

4. Implementation Plan

Participating Service command offices of primary responsibility will review this publication; validate the information; and, where appropriate, reference and incorporate it in Service manuals, regulations, and curricula as follows:

Army. Upon approval and authentication, this publication incorporates the procedures contained herein into the United States (US) Army Doctrine and Training Literature Program as directed by the Commander, US Army Training and Doctrine Command (TRADOC). Distribution is in accordance with applicable directives and the initial distr bution number (IDN) listed on the authentication page.

Marine Corps.[1] The Marine Corps will incorporate the procedures in this publication in US Marine Corps doctrine publications as directed by the Deputy Commandant, Combat Development and Integration (DC, CD&I). Distribution is in accordance with the Marine Corps Publications Distribution System.

Navy. The Navy will incorporate these procedures in US Navy training and doctrine publications as directed by the Commander, Navy Warfare Development Command (NWDC) [N5]. Distribution is in accordance with *Military Standard Requisitioning and Issue Procedure Desk Guide, Naval Supply Systems Command Publication 409.*

Air Force. The Air Force will incorporate the procedures in this publication in accordance with applicable governing directives. Distribution is in accordance with Air Force Instruction 33-360, *Publication and Forms Management.*

Coast Guard. The Coast Guard will incorporate the procedures in this publication as directed by the Commander, Force Readiness Command. Distribution is in accordance with the Coast Guard Directives System. The Coast Guard will utilize the procedures in this publication when operating under the tactical control of Department of Defense. At all other times, the Coast Guard will conduct biometrics in accordance with US Coast Guard standard operating procedures, but will refer to this publication for reference on best practices.

5. User Information

a. US Army Combined Arms Center; Headquarters Marine Corps, DC, CD&I; NWDC; Curtis E. LeMay Center for Doctrine Development and Education (LeMay Center); and the Air Land Sea Application (ALSA) Center developed this publication with the joint participation of the approving Service commands. ALSA will review and update this publication as necessary.

b. This publication reflects current joint and Service doctrine, command and control organizations, facilities, personnel, respons bilities, and procedures. Changes in Service protocol, reflected in joint and Service publications, will be incorporated in revisions to this document.

c. We encourage recommended changes for improving this publication. Key your comments to the specific page and paragraph and provide a rationale for each recommendation. Send comments and recommendations directly to the appropriate Service doctrine centers listed below.

---

[1] Marine Corps PCN: 144 000211 00

Army

Commander, US Army Combined Arms Center
ATTN: ATZL-MCK-D
Fort Leavenworth KS 66027-6900
DSN 552-4885 COMM (913) 684-4885
E-mail: usarmy.leavenworth.mccoe mbx cadd-org-mailbox@mail mil

Marine Corps

Deputy Commandant for Combat Development and Integration
ATTN: C116
3300 Russell Road Suite 204
Quantico VA 22134-5021
DSN 278-3616/6233 COMM (703) 784-3616/6233
E-mail: doctrine@usmc.mil

Navy

Commander, Navy Warfare Development Command
ATTN: N52
1530 Piersey St, Building O-27
Norfolk VA 23511-2723
DSN 341-4185 COMM (757) 341-4185
E-mail: alsapubs@nwdc navy.mil

Air Force

Commander, Curtis E. LeMay Center for Doctrine Development and Education
ATTN: DDJ
401 Chennault Circle
Maxwell AFB AL 36112-6428
DSN 493-7864/1681 COMM (334) 953-7864/1681
E-mail: lemayctr.ddj.wrkflw@us af.mil

Coast Guard

Commander, Force Readiness
US Coast Guard
300 East Main Street
Suite 1100
Norfolk, VA 23510
Comm: (757) 628-4149
E-mail: HQS-SG-M-FORCECOM-TTP-All@uscg.mil

ALSA

Director, ALSA Center
114 Andrews Street
Joint Base Langley-Eustis VA 23665-2785
DSN 575-0902 COMM (757) 225-0902
E-mail: alsa director@langley.af.mil

This page intentionally left blank.

ATP 2-22.85
MCRP 3-33.1J
NTTP 3-07.16
AFTTP 3-2.85
CGTTP 3-93.6

ATP 2-22.85   US Army Combined Arms Center
Fort Leavenworth, Kansas

MCRP 3-33.1J   Headquarters, USMC, Deputy Commandant, CD&I
Quantico, Virginia

NTTP 3-07.16   Navy Warfare Development Command
Norfolk, Virginia

AFTTP 3-2.85   Curtis E. LeMay Center for Doctrine
Development and Education
Maxwell AFB, Alabama

CGTTP 3-93.6   US Coast Guard Force Readiness Command
Norfolk, Virginia

1 April 2014

BIOMETRICS
MULTI-SERVICE TACTICS, TECHNIQUES, AND PROCEDURES FOR
TACTICAL EMPLOYMENT OF BIOMETRICS IN SUPPORT OF OPERATIONS

List of Figures

List of Tables

This page intentionally left blank.

EXECUTIVE SUMMARY
BIOMETRICS

Multi-Service Tactics, Techniques, and Procedures (MTTP) for Tactical Employment of Biometrics in Support of Operations establishes TTP for the proper collection of biometrics in a tactical environment and addresses the importance of quality biometrics enrollments and their applicability to the range of military operations.

Chapter I Overview of Biometrics

Chapter I provides an overview of the primary biometrics modalities collected by Department of Defense and Department of Homeland Security personnel; basic explanation of the biometrics process; and familiarization with the biometrically enabled watchlist (BEWL).

Chapter II Tactical Roles and Responsibilities

Chapter II highlights key roles, responsibilities and planning considerations for leadership and operators to effectively integrate biometrics collection into operations.

Chapter III Biometrics Employment

Chapter III discusses integrating biometrics across the range of military operations.

Chapter IV Biometrics Collection

Chapter IV provides specific TTP for properly collecting quality biometrics data.

Appendix A Negative Data Quality Trends

Appendix A provides examples of improperly collected biometrics.

Appendix B Overview of Current Collection Devices

Appendix B provides an overview of the capabilities of the most common biometrics collection devices currently fielded.

Appendix C Alternate Biometrics Collection Methods

Appendix C provides examples of alternate methods of collecting biometrics data in the event of primary collection device failure or lack of availability.

Appendix D Lessons Learned

Appendix D discusses various techniques used to effectively overcome the challenges of biometrics collection in austere environments.

Appendix E Biometrics Collection Checklist

Appendix E provides a generic, step-by-step guide to ensure a complete biometrics enrollment is accomplished during operations. Also, it provides a quick reference to the BEWL tiers and the appropriate action for each tier.

PROGRAM PARTICIPANTS

The following commands and agencies participated in developing this publication:

Joint

Joint Chiefs Deputy Director J7, Joint Coalition Warfare, Suffo k, VA
Joint Improvised Explosive Device Defeat Organization, Washington, DC
Northern Command, Colorado Springs, CO
US Africa Command, Stuttgart, Germany
US Special Operations Command, Tampa, FL

Army

Armed Forces DNA Identification Laboratory of Armed Forces Medical Examiner, Dover Air Force Base, MD
Defense Forensics Biometrics Agency, Arlington, VA
National Ground Intelligence Center, Charlottesville, VA
US Army Combined Arms Center, Fort Leavenworth, KS
US Army Training and Support Center, Fort Eustis, VA
US Army Special Operations Command, Fort Bragg, NC
US Army Training and Doctrine Command (TRADOC), Fort Eustis, VA
US Army TRADOC Capability Manager for Biometrics and Forensics

Marine Corps

2nd Law Enforcement Battalion, Camp Lejeune, NC
2nd Tank Battalion, Camp Lejeune, NC
Physical Security Division, Law Enforcement Branch, Corrections Section, Quantico, VA
US Marine Corps Combat Development Command, Quantico, VA
US Marine Corps Criminal Investigation Division, Quantico, VA
Weapons Company, 3rd Battalion, 6th Marines, 2d Marine Division, Camp Lejeune, NC

Navy

Navy Expeditionary Intelligence Command, Dam Neck, VA
Navy Surface Warfare Center, Dahlgren, VA
Navy Warfare Development Command, Norfolk, VA

Air Force

Curtis E. LeMay Center for Doctrine Development and Education, Maxwell Air Force Base, AL
Headquarters, Air Combat Command, SGR, Langley Air Force Base, VA
Headquarters, US Air Force (A7SO), Washington, DC

Coast Guard

Force Readiness Command, Norfo k, VA
Headquarters, US Coast Guard Maritime Law Enforcement), Washington, DC

Other

Office of Biometric Identity Management US Department of Homeland Security, Washington, DC

Chapter I

OVERVIEW OF BIOMETRICS

1. Biometrics

Biometrics is part of the Department of Defense's (DOD's) effort to gain identity dominance across the range of military operations (ROMO). Some of the effects include stripping the enemy of anonymity, separating the enemy from the populace, promoting security and governance, denying freedom of movement, mapping the human environment, enhancing force protection and access to facilities, and supporting the identification and targeting of persons of interest and networks.

a. Uses of biometrics.

(1) Verification. This is a task where the biometrics system attempts to confirm an individual's claimed identity by comparing a submitted sample to one or more previously enrolled templates.

(2) Identification. This is a task where the biometrics system searches a database for a reference matching a submitted biometrics sample and, if found, returns a corresponding identity.

b. Modality. This is a type or class of biometrics sample taken from an individual. No single biometrics modality is best for all implementations because many factors must be accounted for when using a biometrics collection device. The primary biometrics modalities collected by the DOD include: facial image, fingerprint, iris scan, deoxyribonucleic acid (DNA), and palm print.

(1) Facial image. Facial images cannot be relied upon as a sole modality for matching identities, but can help when other biometrics and contextual information is available. The picture taken today may contribute to identifying someone tomorrow.

(2) Fingerprint. The most critical element in fingerprinting is collecting the highest quality print. Whenever possible, rolled fingerprints are preferred because they capture more fingerprint surface resulting in a greater chance of matching against latent prints and previously stored fingerprint cards. The higher the quality, the greater the chance a match will be made against a previously collected and stored, latent or live print. When a 10-print card is submitted to the DOD Automated Biometric Identification System (ABIS), a list of candidates who match the submission can be generated. The same is true when latent prints are submitted. Latent print examiners are needed to confirm positive matches.

(3) Iris. Iris recognition is most useful when verifying the identity of an enrolled individual.

(4) DNA. DNA is collected and submitted to a laboratory for analysis. While not as rapid as other biometrics comparisons, DNA is very accurate in person of interest identification and linking individuals to a location, event, or device.

(5) Palm print. A palm print consists of a writer edge (i.e., knife edge) and ball of palm (i.e., front edge). The writer edge is from the wrist bone to the tip of the pinkie. The ball of palm is from the wrist along the thumb line to the tip of the index finger. Currently, the automated biometrics devices discussed in this multi-Service tactics, techniques, and procedures publication do not collect palm prints. Palm prints are collected through a manual process.

2. Overview of the Biometrics Process

The biometrics process involves collecting, matching, storing, analyzing, and sharing biometrics identifiers and associated information of an individual. This methodology is critical to achieving biometrics success and contributes to identity intelligence. Its inclusion is strongly recommended in the military decision making and planning processes, beginning at mission receipt and concluding with after-action reporting.

a. Collect. Collecting consists of capturing a biometrics sample (e.g., facial image, fingerprint, iris image, DNA, or palm print) and related contextual data from an individual using a biometrics collection device. Collection methods may include various forensics techniques to obtain biometrics samples that may be matched against other data.

b. Match. The match function begins as collected biometrics are compared with biometrics records stored on a collection system, or the receipt of a collected biometrics from the Automated Fingerprint Identification System or the DOD ABIS. Depending on the collection device, the collector may be notified with a match/no-match alert banner on the device when the match function is complete.

c. Store. The storage process consists of maintaining and updating biometrics files in databases and ensuring the data is transferred through a network of servers to larger data centers in a theater storage node and, ultimately, to a national database.

d. Analyze. The analyze function incorporates information obtained from biometrics collection activities, forensic operations, and intelligence sources to "connect the dots" during the military decision making process. Biometrics collection is a contributor to this function.

e. Share. The share function is the exchange of biometrics files (i.e., biometrics samples, biographic, and contextual data) and match results with DOD, other federal agencies, and non-federal biometrics partners.

3. Biometrically Enabled Watchlist (BEWL)

a. BEWLs identify persons of interest using biometric samples that are fused with unclassified intelligence information describing each subject, and recommended actions to take if a subject is encountered.

b. The DOD BEWL is the master BEWL within DOD. It lists a large number of identities including known or suspected terrorists, national security threats, and other persons of interest. A search of DOD ABIS includes a search of the entire DOD BEWL.

c. The full DOD BEWL is too large to fit on hand held collection devices such as the Secure Electronic Enrollment Kit II (SEEK II) and Handheld Interagency Identity Detection Equipment (HIIDE), in its entirety. To address the size limitation, subsets of the DOD BEWL, or mission specific BEWLs, are developed and customized for specific operations. The mission specific BEWLs may be loaded onto hand held collection devices, allowing an immediate alert to be triggered if the sought after individuals are encountered during identification or verification operations.

d. The DOD and mission specific BEWLs change over time as subjects' records are added, removed, or updated to include new information. The recurring changes make it important to load the most current version of a BEWL onto hand held collection devices.

e. Historically, BEWLs have been organized into six tiers, each providing a different course of action to be taken by the unit conducting the screening or enrollment. The tiers are as follows.

(1) Tier 1: Detain.

(2) Tier 2: Question (Contact higher authority for guidance.).

(3) Tier 3: Assess.

(4) Tier 4: Do not hire, deny base access, disqualify for police or military training.

(5) Tier 5: Deny base access.

(6) Tier 6: Track movement (Contact higher authority for guidance and follow instructions on the device, if provided.).

f. BEWLs are becoming category-based; each identity on a BEWL can be associated with one or more categories. Each of the six tiers exists as a category. This allows the alert information to include recommended actions and includes additional descriptive categories that may provide information about the subject or DOD's interest in his or her identity.

This page intentionally left blank.

Chapter II
TACTICAL ROLES AND RESPONSIBILITIES

1. Leadership

Leaders play an integral part in biometrics operational success by ensuring biometrics are leveraged to the fullest extent possible to defeat the enemy and enhance protection. It is imperative leaders and collectors understand biometrics data may be used globally across all components of the Federal Government and with international partners. They also must ensure biometrics operations are not treated as a "check-the-block" activity. Quality biometrics collections will lead to a greater degree of force protection for individual units and across the operational environment. High quality collections result in an efficient and cred ble database that requires less effort from managers to correct discrepancies, and increases the likelihood of successful matches. Leadership can support biometrics by:

a. Ensuring that training, operational planning, and execution incorporate biometrics processes and proven tactics, techniques, and procedures.

b. Stressing standardized collection techniques throughout the biometrics community so analysts and decision makers can access cred ble data. An improper biometrics collection wastes time and leads to gaps in knowledge, creating seams that may be exploited by the enemy.

c. Providing feedback to collectors on the impact of their collections at tactical, operational, and strategic levels.

d. Referencing rules of engagement (ROE), staff judge advocate, and command guidance. Prior to conducting operations involving biometrics collection, leaders should review the commander's guidance for updates to legal aspects, ROE, host nation laws, and other legal and cultural considerations. Leaders should consult their servicing legal advisors whenever an operation involves, or is expected to involve, collection from a United States (US) citizen, as US law and/or regulations may limit the collection of biometric identifiers and associated information from US citizens. Leaders must ensure collectors understand the applicable constraints and limitations prior to conducting operations involving biometrics collection.

e. Considering proper site selection for biometrics enrollment operations. Biometrics enrollments in a tactical environment are difficult because of the constraints of time and personnel available.

(1) Select a location that supports the flow of personnel, type of operation, security risks, biometrics task (identification or verification), expected number of operators/collectors and enrollees, user circumstances, existing data, type and amount of equipment, etc. See figure 1 for an example of an enrollment site and operations flow.

(2) Select a location that reduces the environmental impacts of dust, sunlight, and other factors that can limit or prevent the successful biometics collection because they may interfere with the equipment's ability to record data.

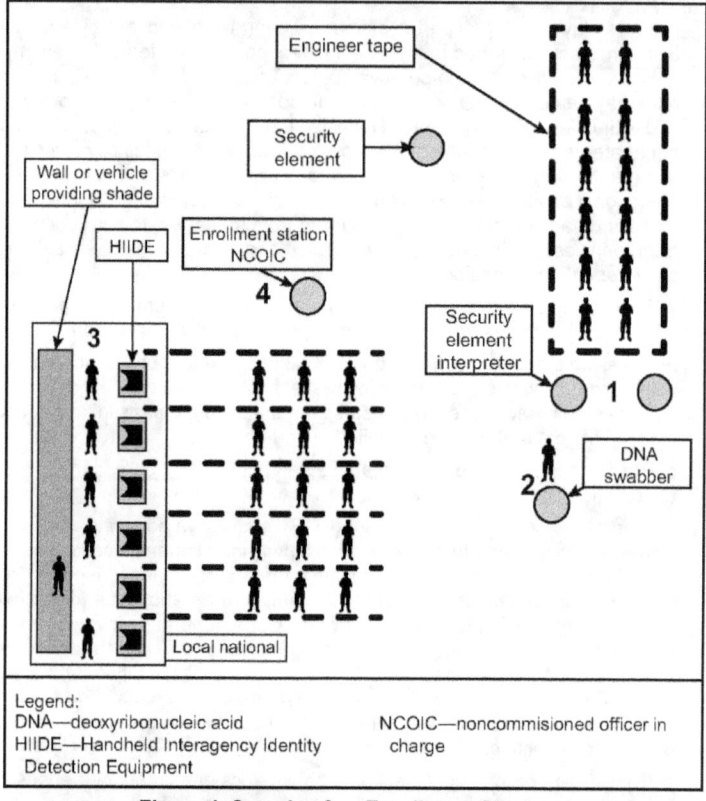

Figure 1. Sample of an Enrollment Site

(3) Ensure adequate network communications are requested and available to support timely biometrics submissions and responses. Consider the time required to establish connectivity.

f. Including biometrics operations in the unit's pre-execution checklist. This ensures all collection devices are loaded with the most up-to-date BEWL, according to the unit's standard operating procedures (SOPs) and as operations dictate. Update the BEWL on devices daily. This is optimal. Weekly updates are the minimum.

g. Working closely with the host nation in the unit's area of operations and gaining acceptance and support of biometrics enrollment operations. If possible, ensure a trained female operator is in view of biometrics collection stations, to facilitate working with female local nationals.

h. Referencing and understanding the biometric collection guidance within the Office of the Secretary of Defense (OSD) memo 14940-11: Authority to collect, store, and share biometric information of non-US persons with US government entities and partner nations, dated 13 Jan 2012 for DOD policy on the authority of military personnel to collect, store, enroll, share, compare, and analyze biometrics information from non-US persons across the full ROMO.

2. Collectors

a. Almost every operation provides the opportunity to collect biometrics. When operators/collectors are trained on the biometrics collection equipment and allowed to collect samples, they become faster and more efficient. This in turn equates to higher quality, and quantity, enrollments. While quality is desired over quantity, maximizing enrollments in the database will likely identify more persons of interest. Efficiency also supports force protection since most small units are vulnerable during collection efforts.

b. Pre-combat checks are essential for biometrics collection success. These can include equipment function checks, current BEWL, adequate power and charge, etc. Maintaining a current BEWL on biometrics collection devices (e.g., Biometric Automated Toolset (BAT), HIIDE, or SEEK II) cannot be over-emphasized. Commanders and operators should ensure current BEWLs are loaded onto DOD-approved biometrics collection equipment.

c. Collect complete, quality, data which includes the biographical and contextual data at every opportunity as the tactical circumstances allow. (This is the who, what, where, when, and why of an encounter, including a person's address, marital status, etc.) Collecting the contextual data and geographical coordinates is essential to ensure the data is complete and provides better context for future applications. Complete enrollments are fundamental to the biometrics process. While complete collection is not always possible, the collection of some quality data is better than having no data at all. See appendix E for a sample checklist.

d. Conduct post-combat checks as soon as possible and ensure all new enrollments are uploaded to the network or submitted to the authoritative database. This ensures the new collections are matched, stored, and shared at the national level and allows for matching against newly processed latent prints. Watchlist data should also be updated at this time, if feasible, to prepare for the next mission requiring biometrics collection. Ensure preventive maintenance services and checks are complete, such as cleaning equipment, charging batteries, and reporting equipment issues are conducted after operations. See appendix E for a sample checklist.

e. For further clarification on the authority to employ biometrics capabilities by combatant commanders and military departments, see OSD memo 14940-11 dated 13 January 2012. DOD Directive 8521.01E: Department of defense biometrics establishes policy, assigns responsibilities, and describes procedures for all DOD biometrics activities.

Chapter III
BIOMETRICS EMPLOYMENT

1. Employment

Biometrics can assist in verifying or identifying friendlies, enemies, or persons of unknown intent by stripping them of anonymity across the ROMO. See figure 2 for examples of these applications.

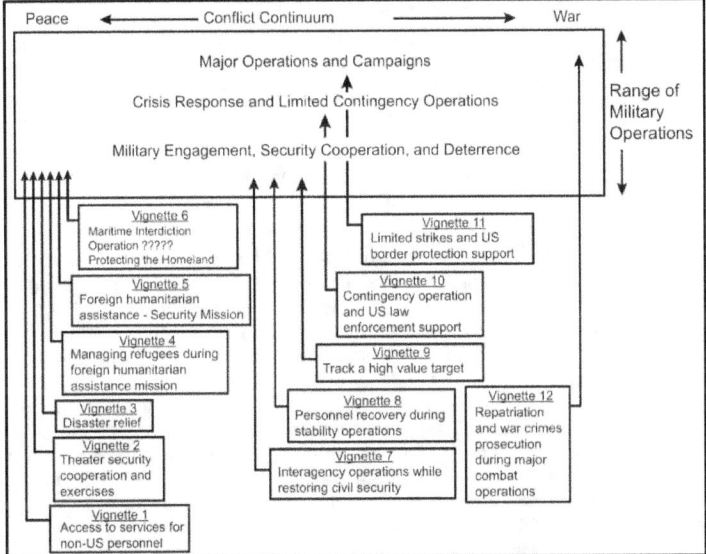

Figure 2. Uses of Biometrics Across the ROMO

2. Mission Types

a. The specific mission types described in this chapter are NOT all inclusive as some missions may fall under multiple operational categories.

b. Depending on the mission, employing biometrics collection and using a DOD authoritative database (such as DOD ABIS) fall into the following six operational categories:

    (1) Combat operations.

        (a) Checkpoint or cordon and search. Enables identification of enrolled residents and identifies transients and unknown biometric identities (UBIs). A UBI is a collected biometrics sample for which there is no known match. This occurs when a sample is collected from an individual who has never been enrolled in the database or a sample has been collected and uploaded from the exploitation of a site.

(b) Targeted or raid. Provides identity confirmation of known targets, associates, and casualties.

(2) Support Operations.

(a) Counter-narcotics. Identifies persons involved in manufacturing, transporting, and distributing narcotics.

(b) Counter-piracy. Identifies parties involved in piracy and tracks their movements.

(c) Detainee operations. Provides identity verification (i.e., determines if people are who they claim to be), and tracking throughout the detainee management process.

(d) Census operations. Provides general population enrollment in combat zones or specific areas of interest to populate databases.

(e) Host nation support. Provides biometrics identification to support civil and military assistance across the ROMO. Building a host nation's capability is a primary factor that encourages information sharing. Security cooperation personnel should aggressively seek to include biometrics in engagements and bi-lateral exercises. Information from host nations may be the biggest source of biometrics collections data. Also, sharing information with host nations requires formal agreements which ensure collection of biometrics from their citizens is not restricted or prohibited by their laws. Biometrics information obtained from a host nation, while extremely valuable, should neither be relied upon as the sole means to populate US or coalition databases, nor used as the sole means to validate a local national's identity. Host nation biometric data may not be available in a relevant time frame; therefore, entering biometric data into US systems for persons known to have been entered in host nation systems is not necessarily redundant.

(3) Humanitarian assistance.

(a) Manage humanitarian aid. Ensures the right individuals receive the right aid and do not "double dip".

(b) Population management. Identifies and monitors movement of the local population.

(c) Non-combatant evacuation operations. Identifies, tracks, and relocates evacuees.

(d) Medical operations. Identifies patients to properly account for resources, ensure they receive appropriate treatment, and families are reunited after a disaster.

(4) Border Control.

(a) Undocumented individuals interdiction. Biometrics enrollment allows identification and tracking of unknown or wanted persons.

(b) Entry control. Verifies the identity of individuals attempting to enter limited-access areas.

(c) Alien migrant interdiction operations. Collects biometrics at sea to process individuals and make prosecution or repatriation decisions.

(5) Intelligence.

(a) Intelligence preparation of the battlespace (IPB). Incorporates biometrics data into the IPB process and produces products (such as, named areas of interest) to use for determining the best locations to collect biometrics data.

(b) BEWL. Provides biometrics data files that are linked to persons of interest and are used to support tactical and strategic operations involving the identification of individuals. Conducting enrollments offers the possibility of getting a "hit" on an individual on a watchlist which can lead to the removal of enemy forces and reducing threats to the operator.

(c) Attacking the network operations. Networks may operate from within the local population in an irregular manner, without a defined identity, and employing guerrilla tactics. Networks are composed of both people and material; therefore, network parts can be identified and targeted using biometrics collection to deny anonymity to the adversary.

(d) Counter-improvised explosive device (IED) operations. Proper enrollments by the operator allow latent-print examiners to match biometrics residue and latent fingerprints to individuals, such as IED emplacers and makers.

(e) Human intelligence (HUMINT), counter-intelligence (CI), and source vetting. Biometrics collection capabilities significantly aid in human screening by verifying the identities of those screened. HUMINT and CI screening are conducted at all echelons of command and in all operational environments.

(6) Force Protection.

(a) Base access. Identifies persons who desire access to a given facility, base, or port; turns away those who have been denied access, and detains persons who are linked to a criminal or terrorist incident.

(b) Personnel vetting. Screens employed persons and local nationals providing contract services which aids in the vetting process, enhances operational area security, and denies access to undesirable personnel and limits the flow of funds to insurgent and terrorist groups.

This page intentionally left blank.

Chapter IV
BIOMETRICS COLLECTION

1. Facial Images

This is the first of four primary biometrics collected in support of operations. The following is required to ensure the proper collection of a facial image:

a. Use a clean and neutral background showing no additional personnel or maps, equipment, vehicles, vessels, etc.

b. Do not allow the person to wear any glasses or other items obscuring the area being photographed. The person may choose to expose only the area from ear to ear and hairline to chin (i.e., they do not have to remove a headdress). There are no constraints on cosmetics.

c. Include the subject's image from the top of the head to the bottom of the neck, including the ears (e.g., passport or identification (ID) card sized photos). See figure 3 for proper alignment and orientation of facial images. Criminal enrollment requires photos that include front, right and left profile, and right and left 45-degree angled images.

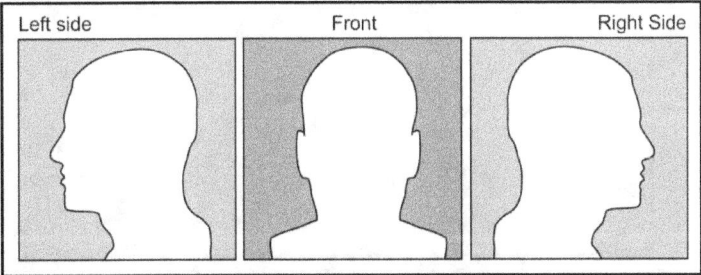

Figure 3. Proper Alignment and Orientation of Facial Images

d. Capture the subject's face expressionless and with the mouth closed and eyes open.

e. Ensure the subject's face is free of shadows and is not in direct light. Improper lighting will create shadows, and direct light will create a shine on the subject's face.

f. Ensure the camera is level and the subject's face is positioned straight and postured toward the camera to ensure a useful front facing photograph. Generally, have the camera lens at subject's nose height to prevent distortion.

g. Capture both profile pictures in the same manner as in paragraph f, except the person should face right (or left) with his or her head facing in the direction of the body.

h. To capture a subject's facial image during low light conditions or at night, supplemental light sources should be placed approximately 45 degrees off the center of the subject's face and pointed at the subject's chest. See figure 4 for an example of how to capture facial images in low-light conditions.

Note: It is important to aim the light source from a 45 degree angle at the subject's chest to prevent the corona of the light from creating a shine on the face.

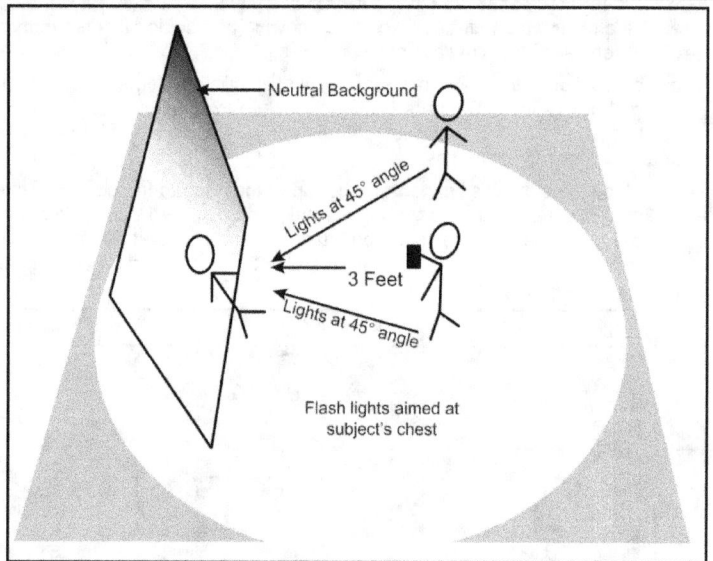

Figure 4. Low-Light Facial Image Capture

2. Electronic Fingerprint Collection

A proper fingerprint should be complete, free of smears, and show friction ridges. See figure 5 for an example of a proper fingerprint. To ensure proper fingerprint collection, the following is required:

a. Ensure the subject's fingers and collection surface are clean prior to collection. Excessive dirt, grease, and dryness of the print area will likely result in an unreadable fingerprint capture. The following is information about the silicone platen.

   (1) Silicone platen must be cleaned to remove residual fingerprints. Unlike glass platen, cleaning the fingerprint silicone membrane does not require a liquid cleaner or special cloth. Instead, apply a small piece of clear tape to the silicone membrane while it is in place atop the platen. This will lift off residual fingerprint images, dirt, oils, and other debris effectively and quickly.

Figure 5. Examples of Proper Slap Prints

(2) The silicone membrane greatly increases the intimate contact area for friction ridge image capture. The silicone surface enables the easy and rapid capturing of fine, worn, and dry finger ridge detail.

b. Maintain control of subject's finger to include slight and consistent pressure for a slap or rolled fingerprint. Look at the print on screen to ensure it is clear. See figure 6 for an example of a method to control the subject, and a proper display on a screen using the SEEK II.

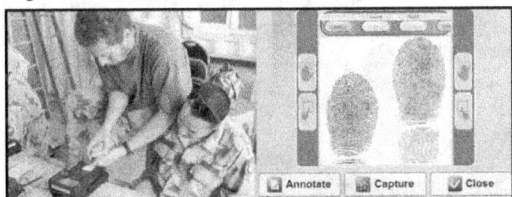

Figure 6. Proper Finger Control and SEEK II Display

c. When collecting rolled fingerprints, roll the subject's finger from knuckle in to knuckle out and from nail in to nail out (i.e., from the subject's uncomfortable position to comfortable position). Thumbs are rolled towards the subject's body, while fingers are rolled away from subject's body. See figure 7 for proper roll direction and figure 8 for an example of a SEEK II display. Rolled prints are always preferred and should be collected whenever poss ble.

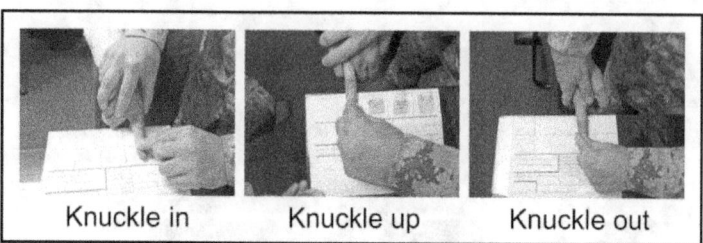

| Knuckle in | Knuckle up | Knuckle out |

Figure 7. Proper Finger Roll Directions

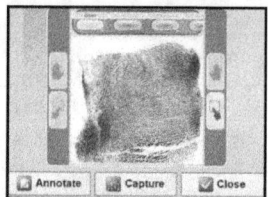

Figure 8. SEEK II Rolled Print Example

3. Iris

The captured image should show the iris and pupil to the maximum extent possible with no glare obscuring any part of the iris. See figure 9 for an example of a proper iris image. The following are required to ensure proper collection of an iris capture.

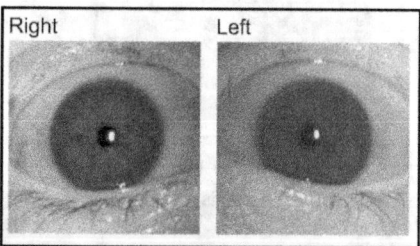

Figure 9. Proper Iris Image

a. Remove any obstructions from the subject's iris, including glasses, contact lenses, eyelashes, hair, etc.

b. Provide a stable position for the subject's head to prevent movement. See figure 10 for proper position for SEEK II and HIIDE iris captures.

Figure 10. SEEK II and HIIDE Iris Captures

c. Subject's eyelids should be open to the maximum extent possible.

d. Subject should STARE FORWARD and REMAIN STILL to avoid excessive eye movement.

e. Avoid direct light that may place a glare over the iris.

4. DNA

DNA may be obtained from an inner cheek, bodily fluids, etc. DNA is very sensitive to contamination, which would render samples useless. If possible, secure collected DNA sample in a clean, sterile, container immediately after collection. The collector should ensure DNA is properly collected by adhering to the following directions.

a. Wear latex gloves to avoid contact with the sample. Do not let samples come in contact with each other.

b. Use a sterile DNA swab to collect a sample from the subject's inner cheek or other source for bodily fluids (i.e., blood). Use the swab on only one person. If swabbing the cheek, tear off one end of the packaging, remove the swab, and keep the packaging. Insert the swab against the inside of the individual's cheek. Move the swab up and down while gently rolling the swab against the cheek for at least 15 seconds. Collect minimal saliva. See figure 11.

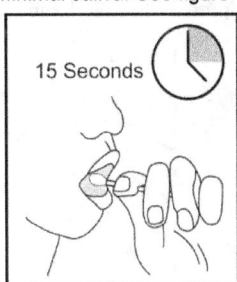

Figure 11. Cheek Swab

c. Try to collect bodily fluids from an uncontaminated area on the subject's body. See figure 12.

d. If time permits, allow the sample to dry in open air for one minute before placing it in a container. Avoid putting the sample into a plastic bag or returning the swab to a culture media tube to prevent degradation due to moisture by mold, fungus, or bacterial growth. Instead, put the evidence into a clean paper bag, envelope, or the original paper swab packaging. Line the container with a blank sheet of paper to prevent fluids from leaking through onto other samples. Place only one individual's sample in a container to avoid cross-contamination of samples. Use tape, not staples, to secure the container. Store DNA samples in a cool, dark, dry place until shipped. When sending DNA samples to a lab, always use paper products to ship the samples. This allows continued drying of the sample. See figure 13. Follow the unit's SOP for shipping DNA samples to a lab.

Figure 12. Bodily Fluid Collection

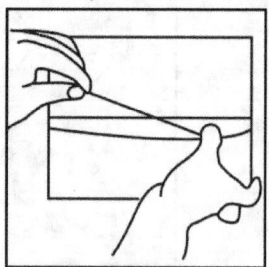

Figure 13. DNA Sample Storage

e. Ensure samples are associated with a specific individual (i.e., name, global unique identifier, electronic fingerprint transaction (EFT), or individual tracking number) and are stored individually and separately.

5. Palm Print

a. The palm print card is a supplement to the criminal or civil fingerprint card and is not intended to stand alone from the actual fingerprint card. Palm prints should be complete, free of smears, and show friction ridges. Figures 14-17 demonstrate the proper locations to ink the palm and proper palm captures on the palm print and supplemental palm print cards.

b. Palm prints are collected using black roller ink, a palm print card (FD-884), and a supplemental finger and palm print card (FD-884a). Each palm will require its own set of cards.

Note: Operators must be trained and proficient in the collection of wet ink fingerprinting for this to be a viable option.

c. Ensure the subject's fingers and collection surface are clean prior to collecting palm prints. Excessive dirt, grease, or dryness of the print area will likely result in an unreadable print.

d. Completing a palm print card.

(1) Roll a coat of black ink along the writer's palm of the hand (also called the ulner side, as in figure 14) from the base of wrist to the fingertip and roll writer's palm impression within capture block.

(2) Roll a coat of ink on the index finger and capture a print in the appropriate block. This print will match and verify the palm print with the ten print fingerprint card.

(3) Roll a coat of ink on the entire palm and fingers (from the base of wrist to finger tips), capturing a print in the appropriate box. Ensure the captured print mirrors the palm illustration in capture box.

(4) Complete the back of the card by rolling fingers in the same manner used on ten print cards.

Note: It is recommended to complete both hand palm prints on their respective cards prior to rolling prints on the reverse side of each card, thus avoiding smudging.

(5) Repeat for the other palm.

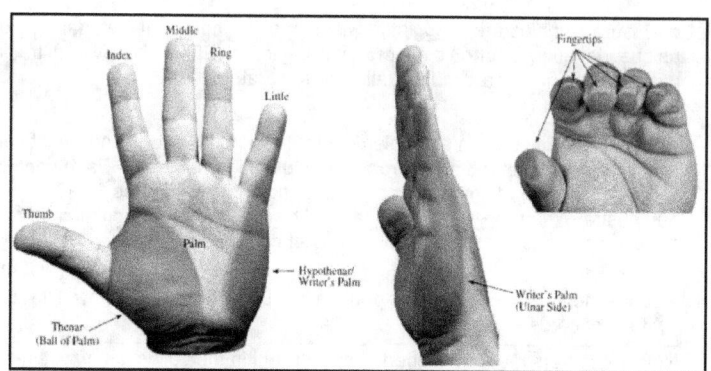

Figure 14. Wet Ink Palm Capture Areas

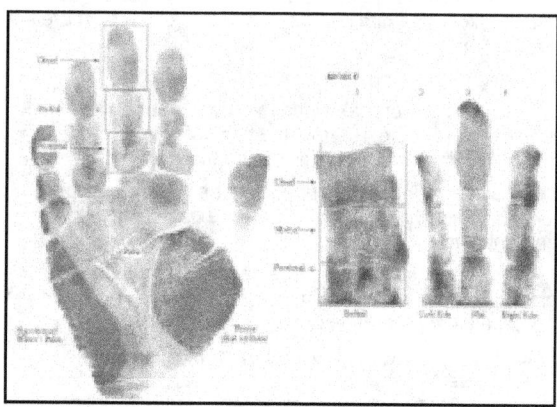

Figure 15. Hand with Basic Ink Regions

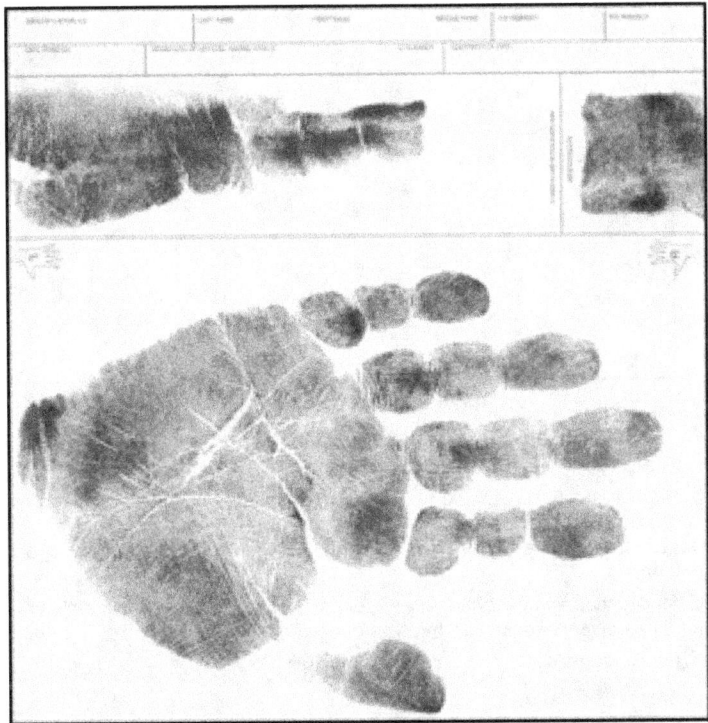

Figure 16. Wet Ink Palm Capture

e. Completing the supplemental finger and palm print cards.

(1) Select left or right hand and check appropriate box.

(2) Ink the appropriate portion of the palm.

(3) Capture the print oriented in the direction of the text (and hand image) within each capture block. Each impression must be captured fully within the box provided, in a vertical, upright position.

(4) The impressions for each digit must be captured: fully rolled, left edge, flat, and right edge.

Note: All digits must be captured in the following sequence: fully rolled, left edge, flat, right edge, contain impressions of the distal, medial and proximal portions of each finger.

(5) Repeat the process for opposite hand.

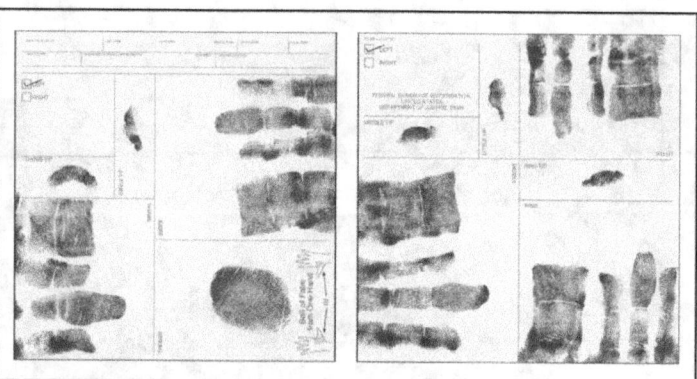

Figure 17. Wet Ink Supplemental Finger and Palm Capture

6. Biographic and Contextual Data

a. The collector should enter accurate and complete information.

b. Names and places should be spelled out phonetically and written in the most accepted manner or based on a transliteration guide. Adherence to a transliteration guide is crucial as it enables name searching within intelligence databases.

c. As situation and guidance dictate, ensure the following information is entered for all enrollments based on the type of enrollment conducted:

    (1) Biographic.

        (a) Name.

        (b) ID number (e.g., passport, national ID, detainee number etc.).

        (c) Phone number.

        (d) Date of birth.

        (e) Place of birth.

        (f) Occupation.

        (g) Gender.

        (h) Place of residence.

        (i) Family members' names.

        (j) Marital status.

        (k) Organization memberships.

        (l) Other names used.

    (2) Contextual.

        (a) Location of encounter (e.g., military grade reference system, grid location, or description of enrollment site).

(b) Reason for enrollment (i.e., person of interest, census, base access, detainee operations).

(c) Date and time enrolled.

7. Uploading the Enrollment

Note: Unit SOPs will determine data uploading responsibility.

a. SEEK II.

(1) Burn enrollment data (i.e., EFT file) onto a compact disc (CD).

(2) Upload data to Service portal or directly to DOD ABIS per SOP.

(3) With multilingual automated registration system software loaded, connect SEEK II to BAT with a crossover cable; BAT transmits data to DOD ABIS.

(4) DOD ABIS will send a "Match-No-Match" response e-mail to the reporting command.

b. HIIDE.

(1) Connect HIIDE to BAT via a crossover cable.

(2) Transfer data from HIIDE to BAT.

(3) BAT transfers data to DOD ABIS.

(4) DOD ABIS will send a "Match-No-Match" response e-mail to the reporting command.

c. BAT.

(1) With connectivity: BAT transfers data to the National Ground Intelligence Center which steps the data down from higher classifications. Only unclassified EFTs are transferred to DOD ABIS.

(2) Without connectivity: Burn data to a CD and locate a BAT with connectivity.

(3) DOD ABIS will send a "Match-No-Match" response e-mail to the reporting command.

This page intentionally left blank.

Appendix A
NEGATIVE DATA QUALITY TRENDS

1. Importance of Accuracy

a. It is imperative to understand the accuracy of the biometrics matching system, the Department of Defense Automated Biometric Identification System (DOD ABIS), is impaired by poor quality biometrics collections. The integrity of DOD ABIS (as a biometrics repository) will be questioned and information derived for warfighter support will be compromised without a well-known, proven, and managed accuracy metric. System speed, throughput, and capacity are critical to warfighter support, but these areas must be properly balanced with biometrics accuracy.

b. Critical to managing biometrics accuracy is ensuring the field capture of biometrics samples is done in a way that preserves the highest quality biometrics while respecting the operational safety of the warfighter and the dignity of the individual providing the biometric data.

2. Persistent Errors

a. The Defense Forensics and Biometrics Agency (DFBA) observed and measured several persistent and systemic errors in the biometrics data within the electronic biometrics transmission specifications files either within or ready to submit to DOD ABIS. The errors include:

(1) Swapped or duplicate fingers between the left and right hand sections of the card.

(2) Swapped hands when referencing the flat-four slaps versus the individual rolled fingers.

(3) A flat fingerprint captured without using the proper technique.

(4) Flat four images captured without all the fingers present.

(5) Rolled fingers that were lifted prematurely.

(6) Facial images marked as a frontal pose that are not a frontal pose.

(7) Iris images captured with a bad technique (i.e., iris scans which have shadowed or mirrored eyes in the images).

(8) Mixed biometrics of multiple subjects (e.g., iris of one subject, fingerprints of another subject).

b. All of these issues degrade the quality of biometrics data sent to DOD ABIS and result in lowering DOD ABIS' capability to match data. DFBA can address some of the issues listed with manual labor, but most of these issues cannot be repaired once the data file is sent to DOD ABIS.

c. See figures 18 through 25 for specific examples of improperly collected biometrics.

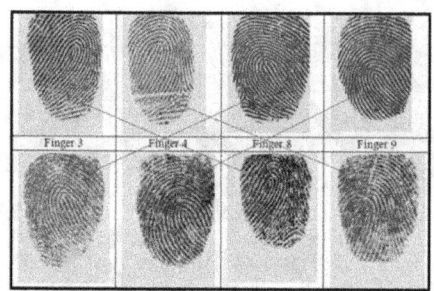

Figure 18. Swapped Hands on a Biometric Automated Toolset Device

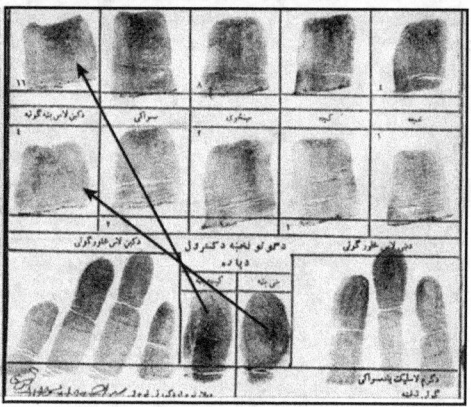

Figure 19. Swapped Thumbs on Scanned Cards

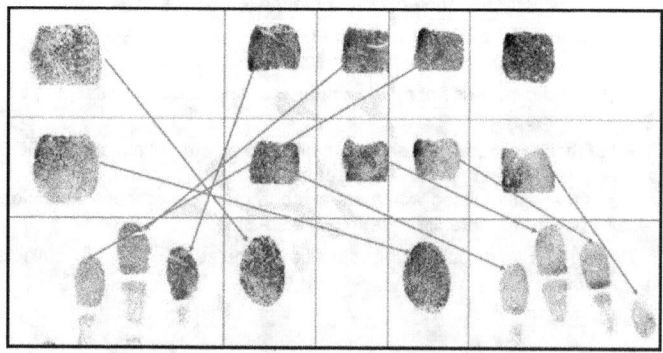

Figure 20. Card with Swapped Fingerprints

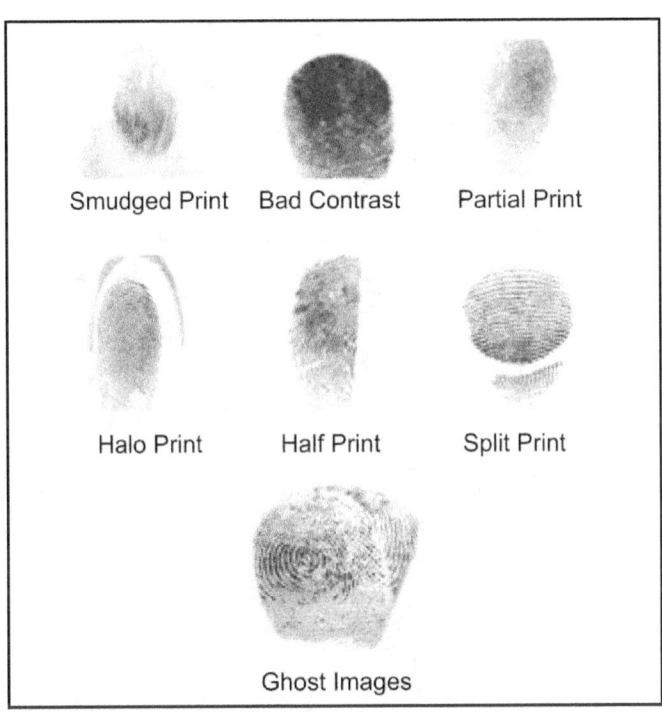

Figure 21. Results of Flat Finger Captures Using Improper Techniques

Figure 22. Flat Four Images Captured Incompletely

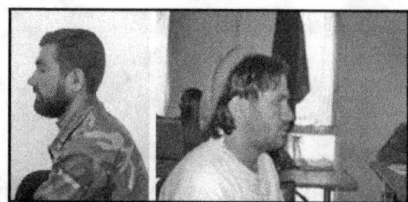

Figure 23. Profile Facial Images Inaccurately Marked as Frontal Poses

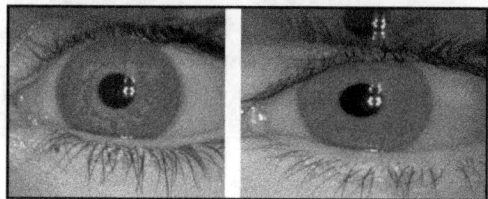

Figure 24. Iris Images with Shadow or Reflection (Mirrored Eyes)

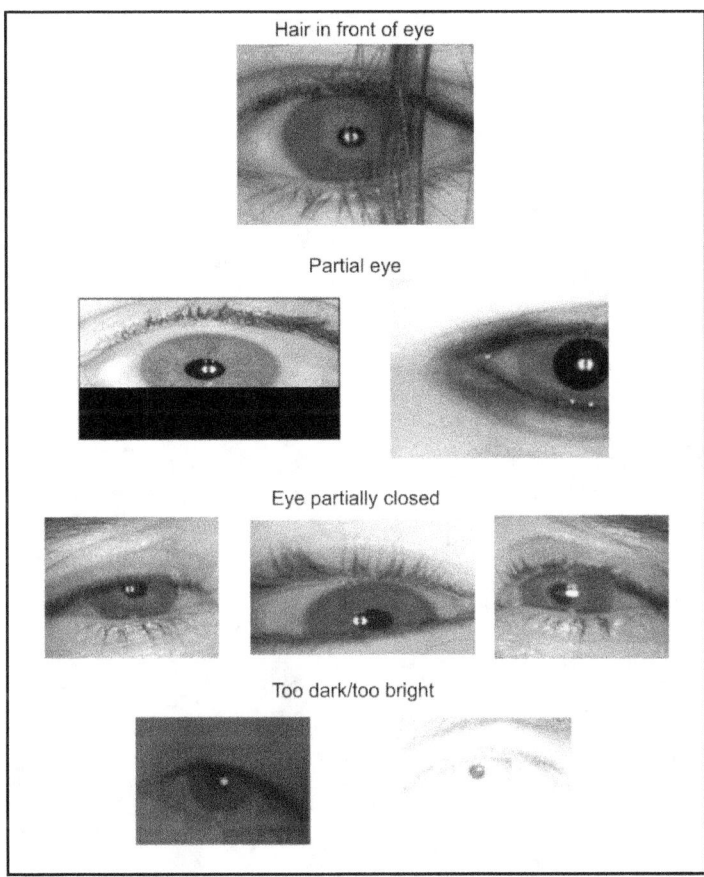

Figure 25. Iris Images Captured Using Bad Techniques

This page intentionally left blank.

Appendix B
DEPARTMENT OF DEFENSE-APPROVED COLLECTION DEVICES

1. Secure Electronic Enrollment Kit II (SEEK II)

a. Function. SEEK II collects fingerprints, iris images, facial photos, and biographical and contextual data of persons of interest and matches fingerprints and iris images against an internal, biometrically enabled watchlist.

b. Characteristics. It is a lightweight (3 pounds (lbs), 6 (ounces) oz), multimodal collection and matching device, compatible with the Department of Defense Automated Biometric Identification System (DOD ABIS), compliant with current software standards, and fully operational in direct sunlight. See figure 26 for an example.

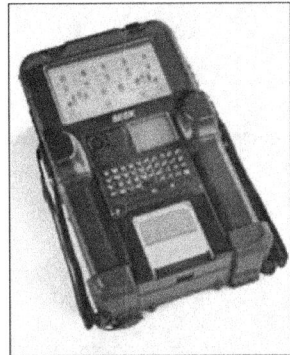

Figure 26. SEEK II

2. Biometric Automated Toolset (BAT)

a. Function. The BAT collects fingerprints, iris scans, facial photos, and biographical information of persons of interest for entry into a searchable data base.

b. Characteristics. It consists of a laptop computer and separate peripherals for collecting biometrics. The toolset system connects to any of the computer servers geographically distributed across an area of operations that store biometrics data. The toolset system is used to identify and track persons of interest and to document and store information about those persons, such as interrogation reports. It is compatible with SEEK II and HIIDE devices. See figure 27 for a photo.

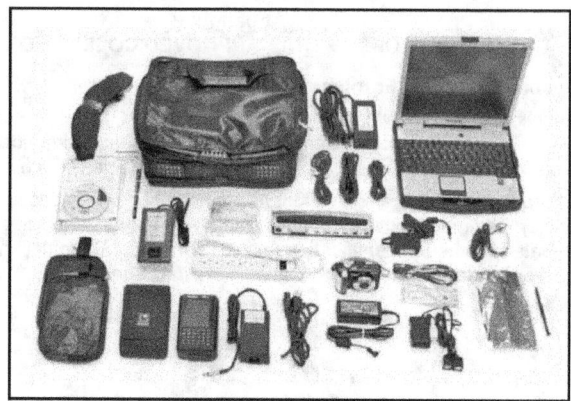

Figure 27. BAT

3. Handheld Interagency Identity Detection Equipment (HIIDE)

a. Function. HIIDE collects fingerprints, iris scans, facial photos, and biographic and contextual data for persons of interest, and matches fingerprints and iris images against an internal watchlist.

b. Characteristics. It is a lightweight (2 lbs, 3 oz), multimodal collection and matching device, compatible with current DOD ABIS software standards. See figure 28 for a picture.

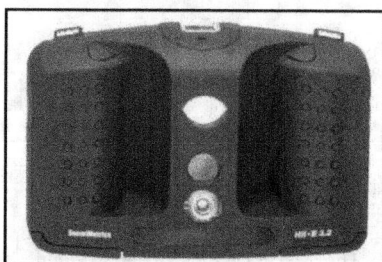

Figure 28. HIIDE

Appendix C
ALTERNATIVE BIOMETRICS COLLECTION METHODS

In the event of electronic biometrics collection device failure, consider the following methods for biometrics collection.

1. Facial Image Capture

a. A standard digital camera can capture a high quality facial image.

b. To aid in facial recognition, a set of "six + 1" pictures can be taken, see figure 29. Tips for successfully taking facial recognition images include the following.

   (1) Use a flash.

   (2) Use a mid-range zoom setting to avoid optical distortion.

   (3) Show a capture tag or name.

   (4) Show ears clearly.

   (5) Remove glasses.

   (6) Position the camera at the subject's nose height for ALL images.

   (7) Avoid causing the subject to squint; use a fill flash if necessary.

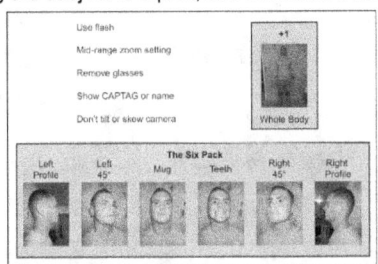

Figure 29. Six Pack + 1 Instruction Card Example

c. Refer to chapter 4, figure 3, for proper collection techniques and illustrations. See figure 30 for an example of a digital camera.

Figure 30. Personal Digital Camera

Note: Using a personal digital camera may be prohibited in the area of operation.

2. Fingerprints

a. Fingerprints can be collected using a black ink pad and a ten-print card (i.e., a card specifically designed for capturing inked fingerprints, such as Form Number-FD 258, a Federal Bureau of Investigation card, or a tactical ten slap card). See figures 31 and 32 for an example of a wet ink capture set and a slap card, respectively. The collector should ensure the quality of the inked print matches the quality on the electronic equipment. Refer to chapter 4 for fingerprint collection techniques and illustrations.

Note: Operators must be trained and proficient in collecting wet ink fingerprints for this to be a viable option.

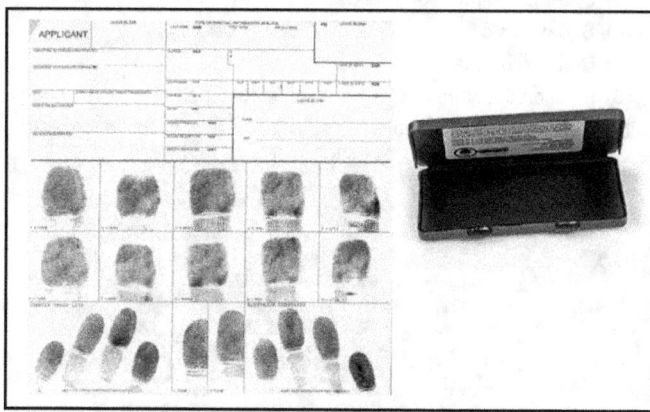

Figure 31. Wet Ink Print Capture Card and Ink Pad

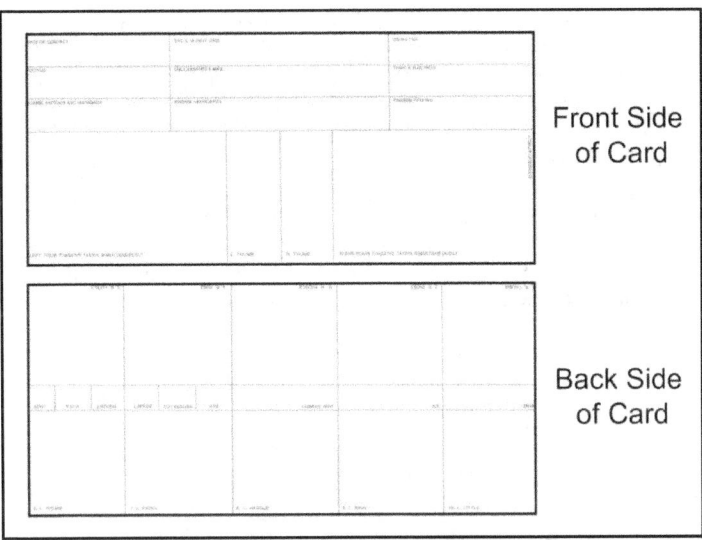

Figure 32. Tactical Ten Slap Card

b. When electronic and ink methods are unavailable, a plain fingerprint impression can be obtained by performing the following steps.

(1) Record on a white piece of paper the name of the subject, time, and date with the grid location on the bottom corner of the paper.

(2) Fold the paper in half.

(3) Have the subjects wipe their fingers lightly across the side of their nose with both hands at least three times to pick up the oil on the skin.

(4) Have the subjects run their hands through their hair three times to pick up the oil in the hair.

(5) Hold the folded paper and have the subjects press their fingertips from both sides onto the paper, making sure to get the tips of the fingers from one-fourth inch below the first joint.

3. Iris

Note: There is no approved alternative collection method for an iris capture.

4. Deoxyribonucleic Acid (DNA)

a. If sterile DNA swabs are unavailable, use a small, sterile gauze pad or sterile, commercial cotton swab to swab the inside of the mouth to capture a viable DNA sample. Refer to chapter 4 to see how to collect a DNA sample.

b. If using a sterile, cotton swab, either swab the individual with both ends of it or indicate on the packaging or swab which end was used to collect the sample.

c. The collection source should be placed back in its packaging or sealed in a non-plastic container for transport. See paragraph 4 of chapter 4 for more information.

5. Contextual Data

a. If there are any biometrics collected using the alternative methods previously discussed, it is imperative to link the contextual information and biometrics record properly.

b. See chapter 4 for specific examples of important contextual data needed to support a complete biometrics enrollment.

Appendix D
LESSONS LEARNED

1. Device and General Issues and Remedies

a. Missing features. It is important to document any factors that prohibit collecting biometrics data (e.g., missing eyes or heavy cataracts, which prohibit conducting an iris scan; or missing fingers, hands, or limbs, which prevent capturing a full set of fingerprints). Additionally, units should enroll subjects in the biometrics database even if they cannot meet specific minimum standards and should not institute local policies which prohibit their biometrics enrollment (e.g., the subject does not have a minimum number of fingerprints to meet standard requirements).

b. Trouble collecting iris scans with secure electronic collection kit (SEEK) II. The subject may try to move his or her head to match SEEK II movement during an iris scan. This issue may be compounded if collection takes place in a rough sea state. The collector may hold the subject's head stationary to allow positioning of the SEEK II for the best collection. Also, the collector may place the subject in a seated position with his or her chin tucked to the chest. This allows the collector to affix the SEEK II over the eyes while helping to eliminate excess motion.

c. Trouble inputting data with a small SEEK II keypad. The small keypad may inh bit quick entry of contextual data into the SEEK II system. This issue is compounded with the use of gloves. An optional universal serial bus-powered rubber roll-up keyboard can be used to mitigate the problem.

d. Trouble collecting facial images during low light or night conditions. Not having enough light or having the light source in a non-ideal location creates poor-quality photographs with excessive shadows (See chapter 4 figures). Move the subject to a secure location where light sources can be controlled or used more effectively. Consider using multiple light sources to mitigate shadows and enable capturing high quality images. Offset the light source by aiming it towards the subject's chest instead of shining it directly onto the subject's face.

e. Trouble with fingerprints not reading. Clean the fingerprint screen and the subject's hands, and rehydrate subject's fingers by having the subject run his or her hands through own hair; or increase pressure on fingerprint pad. If the skin is rough or callused and difficult to print, the hands should be cleaned and, if necessary, soaked in warm water. Soaking softens the skin and brings out the friction ridges. After soaking, the hands should be dried thoroughly, as moisture on the hands will blur the prints.

f. Trouble with blurred fingerprint images. Slipping causes the fingerprints to smudge and blur. Keep positive control and maintain slight pressure on the subject's finger and hand, guiding fingers through the correct movements for an optimal print collection (see figures in chapter 4).

g. Trouble with batteries dying during the mission. Collectors should ensure their collection device is charged prior to and immediately following the mission. Remove batteries when not in use to eliminate battery power depletion.

h. Collecting iris scans from deceased persons. Collect iris scans as soon as practical. It is best to collect iris scans within 30 minutes post-mortem. Environmental conditions can reduce this timeline and render the irises unreadable.

i. Collecting DNA from the deceased. Do not remove limbs or body parts. Collect a DNA sample using the subject's bodily fluids from an uncontaminated area or source.

Note: Updating the biometrically enabled watchlist before each mission on each device increases the likelihood of matching a suspected person of interest.

2. Maritime Issues and Remedies

a. Unstable collection platform. Rough seas and vessel movement may make collecting biometrics difficult while standing. Seat the subject to create a more stable and comfortable position.

b. Trouble collecting iris scans with a SEEK II. The subject may try to move his/her head to match movement of the SEEK II during an iris scan. This issue may be compounded if collection takes place in a rough sea state. The collector may hold the subject's head stationary to allow positioning of the SEEK II for the best collection. Also, the collector may place the subject in a seated position with the chin tucked to the chest. This allows the collector to affix the SEEK II over the eyes while helping to eliminate excess motion.

c. Transporting and storing the electronic biometrics device. Transporting and storing the biometrics device in a waterproof bag before and after use may mitigate the effects of sea spray and inclement weather conditions.

d. Trouble collecting biometrics data. In a rough sea state, bring the vessel on a steady course directly into the sea (i.e., waves and swells should be perpendicular to the vessel's bow) to create a steady state for the subject and biometrics device. Alternatively, a smaller vessel can be positioned in the lee of a larger vessel.

Appendix E
BIOMETRICS COLLECTION CHECKLIST

Table 1 is an example of a biometrics collection checklist.

Table 1. Biometrics Collection Checklist					
Collection Checklist			Tier Levels		
(Minimum required)			Tier 1: Detain		
Facial image	Yes	No	Tier 1: Detain		
	Straight	Side	Tier 2: Question Tier 3: Further Consideration		
			Tier 3: Further Consideration		
Fingerprint	Yes	No	Tier 4: No Hire		
	6	10	Tier 5: Deny Base Access		
			Tier 6: No Action Required		
Iris scan	Yes	No			
DNA	Yes	No			
Contextual data	Yes	No			
Pre-combat check			Post-combat check		
(Not device specific)			(Not device specific)		
Equipment inventory	Yes	No	Equipment inventory	Yes	No
Fully charged batteries	Yes	No	Charge batteries	Yes	No
Extra charged batteries	Yes	No	Download collected data	Yes	No
(Mission dependent)			Clean and prep	Yes	No
Power supply (if needed)	Yes	No	Report equipment failures	Yes	No
Function check	Yes	No			
Uploaded current watchlist	Yes	No			

This page intentionally left blank.

REFERENCES

JOINT PUBLICATIONS

JP 1, *Doctrine for the Armed Forces of the United States*, 20 Mar 2009
JP 1-02, *Department of Defense [DOD] Dictionary of Military and Associated Term*, 8 Nov 2012
DOD Dir. 8521.01E, *Department of Defense Biometrics*, 21 Feb 2008

AIR FORCE PUBLICATIONS

AFDD 3-05, *Special Operations*, 28 Jul 2011

ARMY PUBLICATIONS

Biometrics Identity Management Agency, Biometrics Glossary, Version 6, http://www.biometrics.dod.mil/Files/Documents/Standards/BioGlossary.pdf, April 2012
FM 3-05, *Army Special Operations Forces*, 01 Dec 2010
TC 2-22.82, *Biometrics-Enabled Intelligence*, 03 Mar 2011

MARINE CORPS PUBLICATIONS

MCIP 3-17.02,*MAGTF Counter-Improvised Explosive Device Operations*, 24 Jan 2011
Marine Corps Lessons Learned, *Biometrics Efforts in Afghanistan*, 10 Sep 2012

NAVY PUBLICATIONS

NWP 3-05, *Naval Special Warfare*, May 2013

COAST GUARD

COMDTINST M16247.1F, *US Coast Guard Maritime Law Enforcement Manual (MLEM)*, 26 March 2013

MULTI-SERVICE PUBLICATIONS

ATP 3-09.32, MCRP 3-16.6A, NTTP 3-09.2, AFTTP(I) 3-2.6, *Multi-Service Tactics, Techniques, and Procedures for the Joint Application of Firepower (JFIRE)*, 30 Nov 2012

OTHER PUBLICATIONS

Biometrics Task Force Newsletter, v4 issue 2_a3, http://www.biometrics.dod.mil/Newsletter/issues/2008/Jan/v4issue2/v4Issue2_a3.html, Apr/May/Jun 2008
Crossmatch equipment brochure, http://www.crossmatch.com/seekII.php
Merriam-Webster dictionary, http://www.merriam-webster.com/dictionary/distal
OSD Memo 14940-11, 13 Jan 2012

This page intentionally left blank.

GLOSSARY

A

AFDD	Air Force Doctrine Document
AFB	Air Force Base
AFTTP	Air Force tactics, techniques, and procedures
AFTTP(I)	Air Force tactics, techniques, and procedures (interservice)
ALSA	Air Land Sea Application (Center)
ABIS	Automated Biometric Identification System

B

BAT	Biometric Automated Toolset
BEWL	biometrically enabled watchlist

C

CD&I	Combat Development and Integration
CADD	Combined Arms Doctrine Directorate
CD	compact disc
CGTTP	Coast Guard tactics, techniques, and procedures
CI	counter-intelligence

D

DC	Deputy Commandant
DFBA	Defense Forensics and Biometrics Agency
DNA	deoxyribonucleic acid
DOD	Department of Defense

E

EFT	Electronic Fingerprint Transaction

F, G

FM	field manual

H

HIIDE	handheld interagency identity detection equipment
HUMINT	human intelligence

I

ID	identification
IDN	initial distribution number
IED	improvised explosive device
IPB	intelligence preparation of the battlespace

J, K

JP	joint publication

L

lb	pound
LeMay Center	Curtis E. LeMay Center for Doctrine Development and Education

M

MCRP	Marine Corps reference publication
MTTP	multi-Service tactics, techniques, and procedures

N

NCOIC	noncommissioned officer in charge
NTTP	Navy tactics, techniques, and procedures
NWDC	Navy Warfare Development Command

O, P, Q

OSD	Office of the Secretary of Defense
oz	ounce

R

ROE	rules of engagement
ROMO	range of military operations

S

SEEK II	Secure Electronic Enrollment Kit II
SOP	standard operating procedure

T

TRADOC	United States Army Training and Doctrine Command
TTP	tactics, techniques, and procedures

U, V, W, X, Y, Z

UBI	unknown biometric identities
US	United States

PART II — TERMS AND DEFINITIONS

Arch—A fingerprint pattern in which the friction ridges enter from one side, make a rise in the center, and exit on the opposite side. The pattern will contain no true delta point. (Source: Biometrics Glossary v6).

Automated Biometric Identification System—The central, authoritative, multimodal biometric data repository for DOD. The system operates and enhances associated search and retrieval services and interfaces with existing DOD and interagency biometrics systems. The repository interfaces with collection systems, intelligence systems and other deployed biometric repositories across the federal government. Also called ABIS. (Source: Biometrics Glossary v6).

Automated Fingerprint Identification System (AFIS)—A highly specialized biometric system that compares a submitted fingerprint record (usually of multiple fingers) to a database of records, to determine the identity of an individual. AFIS is predominantly used for law enforcement, but is also being used for civil applications (e.g., background checks for soccer coaches, etc). (Source: Biometrics Glossary v6).

Biographic Data—Data that descr bes physical and non-physical attributes of a biometric subject from whom biometric sample data has been collected. For example, full name, age, height, weight, address, employers, telephone number, e-mail address, birthplace, nationality, education level, group affiliations, also data such as employer, security clearances financial and credit history. (Source: Biometrics Glossary v6).

Biometric—Of or having to do with biometrics. (Source: Biometrics Glossary v6).

Biometrics—A general term used alternatively to describe a characteristic or a process. As a characteristic: The measure of a biological (anatomical and physiological) and/or behavioral biometric characteristic that can be used for automated recognition. As a process: Automated methods of recognizing an individual based on the measure of biological (anatomical and physiological) and/or behavioral biometric characteristics. (Source: Biometrics Glossary v6).

Biometric Automated Toolset (BAT)—A multimodal biometric system that collects and compares fingerprints, iris images and facial photos. It is used to enroll, identify and track persons of interest; build digital dossiers on the individuals that include interrogation reports, biographic information, relationships, etc. (Source: Biometrics Glossary v6).

Biometric Capture Device—A device that collects a signal from a biometric characteristic and converts it to a captured biometric sample. (Source: Biometrics Glossary v6).

Biometric Capture Process—Process of collecting or attempting to collect signals from a biometric characteristic and converting them to a captured biometric sample. (Source: Biometrics Glossary v6).

Biometric Characteristic—A biological and/or behavioral characteristic of a biometric subject that can be detected and from which distinguishing, repeatable biometric features can be extracted for the purpose of automated recognition of biometric subjects. (Source: Biometrics Glossary v6).

Biometric Data—A catch-all phrase for computer data created during a biometric process. It encompasses raw sensor observations, biometric samples, models, templates and/or similarity scores. Biometric data is used to describe the information collected during an enrollment, verification, or identification process, but does not apply to end user information such as user name, demographic information and authorizations. (Source: Biometrics Glossary v6).

Biometric Database—A collection of one or more computer files. For biometric systems, these files could consist of biometric sensor readings, templates, match results, related biometric subject information, etc. (Source: Biometrics Glossary v6).

Biometric Identity—A biometric identity is established when a biometric sample(s) is used instead of a name to identify a Person of Interest (POI). The biometric identity may consist of the results of one or more biometric encounters for the same individual. (Source: Biometrics Glossary v6).

Biometric Information—A catch-all phrase that includes but is not limited to biometric data, contextual data and associated information obtained during the biometric process. (Source: Biometrics Glossary v6).

Biometric Sample—Analog or digital representation of biometric characteristics, or biological specimen prior to biometric feature extraction. (Source: Biometrics Glossary v6).

Biometric Subject—An individual from which biometric samples were collected. (Source: Biometrics Glossary v6).

Biometrically Enabled Watchlist (BEWL)—Any list of persons of interest (POI), with individuals identified by biometric sample instead of by name and the desired/recommended disposition instructions for each individual. (Source: Biometrics Glossary v6).

Collect—The capability and/or process to capture biometric sample(s) and related contextual data from a biometric subject, with or without his or her knowledge. (Source: Biometrics Glossary v6).

Contextual Data—Elements of biographic data and situational information (who, what, when, where, how, why, etc.) associated with a collection event and permanently recorded as an integral component of the biometric file. (Source: Biometrics Glossary v6).

Defense Forensics and Biometrics Agency—DFBA consolidates and coordinates forensics and biometrics activities and operations for the Department of Defense in support of the National Security Strategy. (Source Defense Forensics Biometrics Agency memo).

Delta Point—The part of a fingerprint pattern that looks similar to the Greek letter delta. Technically, it is the point on a friction ridge at or nearest to the point of divergence of two type lines, and located at or directly in front of the point of divergence. (Source: Biometrics Glossary v6).

Distal—Situated away from the point of attachment or origin or a central point especially of the body. (Source: Merriam-Webster dictionary).

DNA Matching—Utilizing DNA to identify a biometric subject. (Source: Biometrics Glossary v6).

Electronic Fingerprint Transmission Specification (EFTS)—A document that specifies requirements to which agencies must adhere to communicate electronically with the Federal Bureau of Investigation (FBI) Integrated Automated Fingerprint Identification System (IAFIS). This specification facilitates information sharing and eliminates the delays associated with fingerprint cards. (Source: Biometrics Glossary v6).

Enroll—Create and store, for a biometric subject, an enrollment data record that includes biometric reference(s) and typically, non-biometric data. (Source: Biometrics Glossary v6).

Face Recognition—A biometric modality that uses an image of the visible physical structure of a biometric subject's face for recognition purposes. (Source: Biometrics Glossary v6).

Fingerprint—The image left by the minute ridges and valleys found on the hand of every person. In the fingers and thumbs, these ridges form patterns of loops, whorls and arches. (Source: Biometrics Glossary v6).

Flat Fingerprint—Fingerprints taken in which the finger is pressed down on a flat surface but not rolled. Also known as Plain Fingerprint. (Source: Biometrics Glossary v6).

Friction Ridge—The ridges present on the skin of the fingers and toes, and on the palms and soles of the feet, which make contact with an incident surface under normal touch. On the fingers, the distinctive patterns formed by the friction ridges that make up the fingerprints. (Source: Biometrics Glossary v6).

Handheld Interagency Identity Detection Equipment—A portable biometric collection device that collects iris, fingerprint and facial data. It can be preloaded with a watchlist for data comparison. A peripheral device to the BAT and provides untethered biometrics verification and in some cases a collection capability. Together the BAT and HIIDE capture, transmit, store, share, retrieve, match, and display biometrics data to identify known persons of interest. (Source: L-1 Identity

Solution brochure; Biometrics Task Force Newsletter, v4 issue 2_a3).

Identity—Identity is a set of characteristics by which an entity (e.g., human, application, device, service or process) is recognizable from every other entity. (Source: Biometrics Glossary v6).

Identity Dominance—Identity Dominance is defined as the operational capability to achieve an advantage over an adversary by denying him the ability to mask his identity and/or to counter our biometric technologies and processes. This is accomplished through the use of enabling technologies and processes to establish the identity of an individual and to establish a knowledge base for that identity. This includes denying an adversary the ability to identify our protected assets. (Source: Biometrics Glossary v6).

Identity Intelligence—Information produced by the discovery, management, and protection of Identity attributes in support of U.S. national and homeland security interests. (Source: Biometrics Glossary v6).

Iris Recognition—A biometric modality that uses an image of the physical structure of a biometric subject's iris for recognition purposes. (Source: Biometrics Glossary v6).

Latent Fingerprint—A fingerprint "image" left on a surface that was touched by a biometric subject. The transferred impression is left by the surface contact with the friction ridges, usually caused by the oily residues produced by the sweat glands in the finger. (Source: Biometrics Glossary v6).

Latent Print—Transferred impression of friction ridge detail not readily visible; generic term used for questioned friction ridge detail. (Source: Biometrics Glossary v6).

Loop—A fingerprint pattern in which the friction ridges enter from either side, curve sharply and pass out near the same side they entered. This pattern will contain one core and one delta. (Source: Biometrics Glossary v6).

Medial—Being or occurring in the middle. (Source: Merriam-Webster dictionary).

Modality—A type or class of biometric sample originating from a biometric subject. For example: face recognition, fingerprint recognition, iris recognition, DNA, etc. (Source: Biometrics Glossary v6).

Palm Print—An exemplar or latent friction ridge image from the palm (side and underside) of the hand. (Source: Biometrics Glossary v6).

Palm Print Recognition—A biometric modality that uses the physical structure of a biometric subject's palm print for recognition purposes. (Source: Biometrics Glossary v6).

Person of Interest (POI)—An individual for whom information needs or discovery objectives exist. (Source: Biometrics Glossary v6).

Plain Fingerprint—Fingerprints taken in which the finger is pressed down on a flat surface but not rolled. Also known as Flat Fingerprint. (Source: Biometrics Glossary v6).

Platen—The surface on which the fingers, toes, palms, or soles of the feet are placed during optical image capture. Platens are also used by other types of electronic fingerprint devices (i.e. capacitive, optical, electro-optical, etc.). (Source: Biometrics Glossary v6).

Proximal—Next to or nearest the point of attachment or origin, a central point, or the point of view; especially: located toward the center of the body. (Source: Merriam-Webster dictionary).

Rolled Fingerprint—An image that includes fingerprint data from nail to nail, obtained by "rolling" the finger across a sensor. (Source: Biometrics Glossary v6).

Secure Electronic Enrollment Kit II—A portable biometric collection device that collects flat and rolled fingerprints, iris and facial images. It has a QWERTY keyboard. The captured data conforms to EBTS standards, enrolls data into AFIS database and compares it against watchlists. Includes 3G communication support with wireless networking capability for remote access to databases such as DOD ABIS. (Source: Crossmatch equipment brochure).

Slap Fingerprint—Fingerprints taken by simultaneously pressing the four fingers of one hand onto a scanner or a fingerprint card. Slaps are known as four finger simultaneous plain impressions. (Source: Biometrics Glossary v6).

Ten (10) Print Match or Identification—An absolute positive identification of a biometric subject by corresponding each of his or her 10 fingerprints to those in a system of record. Usually performed by an AFIS system and verified by a human fingerprint examiner. (Source: Biometrics Glossary v6).

Valley—The area surrounding a friction ridge that does not make contact with an incident surface under normal touch; the area between two friction ridges. (Source: Biometrics Glossary v6).

Whorl—A friction ridge pattern in which the ridges of the fingers, toes, palms, and soles of the feet are circular or nearly circular. The pattern will contain 2 or more deltas. (Source: Biometrics Glossary v6).

This page intentionally left blank.

ATP 2-22.85
MCRP 3-33.1J
NTTP 3-07.16
AFTTP 3-2.85
CGTTP 3-93.6

1 April 2014

By Order of the Secretary of the Army

Official:

RAYMOND T. ODIERNO
General, United States Army
Chief of Staff

GERALD B. O'KEEFE
Administrative Assistant
to the
Secretary of the Army
1402802

DISTRIBUTION:

Active Army, Army National Guard, and US Army Reserve: Distr bute in accordance with the initial distribution number (IDN) 116049, requirements for ATP 2-22.85.

By Order of the Secretary of the Air Force

JAMES A. FIRTH
Brigadier General, US Air Force
Mobilization Assistant to the Commander
Curtis E. LeMay Center for Doctrine
  Development and Education

ACCESSIBILITY: Publications and forms are available on the e—Publishing website at www.e—publishing .af.mil for downloading or ordering.

RELEASABILITY: Distribution approved for public release; distribution is unlimited. This determination was made on 7 January 2014.

MARINE CORPS PCN: 144 000211 00   PIN: 103962-000